growing potatoes

growing potatoes

a directory of varieties and how to cultivate them successfully

Richard Bird
and **Alex Barker**

LORENZ BOOKS

This edition is published by Lorenz Books,
an imprint of Anness Publishing Ltd,
108 Great Russell Street,
London WC1B 3NA;
info@anness.com

www.lorenzbooks.com;
www.annesspublishing.com;
twitter: @Anness_Books

If you like the images in this book
and would like to investigate using
them for publishing, promotions or
advertising, please visit our website
www.practicalpictures.com for
more information.

© Anness Publishing Ltd 2016

All rights reserved. No part of this
publication may be reproduced, stored
in a retrieval system, or transmitted in
any way or by any means, electronic,
mechanical, photocopying, recording
or otherwise, without the prior written
permission of the copyright holder.

A CIP catalogue record for this book
is available from the British Library.

Publisher: Joanna Lorenz
Project Editor: Felicity Forster
Photographers: Jonathan Buckley
    and Steve Moss
Jacket Photographer: Tim Auty
Designer: Louise Kirby
Production Controller: Rosanna Anness

PUBLISHER'S NOTE
Although the advice and information
in this book are believed to be accurate
and true at the time of going to press,
neither the authors nor the publisher can
accept any legal responsibility or liability
for any errors or omissions that may have
been made nor for any inaccuracies nor
for any loss, harm or injury that comes
about from following instructions or
advice in this book.

Contents

Introduction

The potato is a member of the Solanaceae family and is related to both the tomato and the tobacco plant. The only edible part of the plant is the tuber. The potato is the staple food for two-thirds of the world's population and is the third most important food crop in the world. It is an excellent source of nutrients in the diet, including vitamins B and C, and a good provider of protein, as well as complex carbohydrates.

EARLY HISTORY
The potato was discovered by pre-Inca Indians in the foothills of the Andes Mountains in South America. Archaeological remains dating back to 400 BC have been found on the shores of Lake Titicaca, in ruins near Bolivia and on the coast of Peru. Not only did the Incas cultivate the potato, it influenced their whole lives: the Peruvian potato goddess was depicted holding a potato plant in each hand; South American Indians measured time by the length of time it took to cook potatoes to various consistencies; potato designs have been found on Nazca and Chimu pottery; and slices of raw potato placed on the body were used to help heal broken bones and prevent rheumatism.

The original potatoes, which ranged from the size of a nut to that of a small apple and in colour from red or gold to blue or black, flourished in the temperate mountain plateaux. The first recorded information about the potato, by a Spanish conquistador, dates from 1553, and soon potatoes joined the treasures carried to Europe by the Spanish invaders. They also became standard fare on Spanish ships, and it was quickly noticed that sailors who ate them did not suffer from scurvy.

SPREAD OF POPULARITY
The cultivation of potatoes soon spread throughout Europe. Sir Francis Drake is said to have introduced potatoes to Britain, and Sir Walter Raleigh is believed to

BELOW As potatoes grow, it is important to earth (hill) up the plants. This prevents the tubers from being exposed to sunlight, which makes them green and inedible.

have grown them on his estates in Ireland. Botanists and scientists were fascinated by this novel plant, and it may have been grown mainly for botanical research. In the 17th century the Royal Society recognized it as both nutritious and inexpensive, and with the ever-present fear of famine and war, governments throughout Europe encouraged farmers to start growing this useful crop. Frederick II of Prussia ordered his people to plant potatoes to prevent famine and enforced his order by threatening to cut off the noses and ears of those who refused.

By the end of the 18th century the potato was a major food crop, particularly in Germany and Britain, and it has been estimated that Irish peasants were eating a daily average of 10 potatoes each, representing 80 per cent of their diet. In addition, potatoes were fodder for their animals. This dependence proved disastrous when potato blight struck the harvest in three successive years in the 1840s. More than a million people died, and many more than that number emigrated in desperation.

European immigrants originally introduced the potato to North America, but it was not until Irish immigrants brought the potato to Londonderry, New Hampshire, in the early 18th century that it began to be grown in quantity. In the following century, Lord Selkirk emigrated with a group from Scotland and settled an area known as Orwell Point on Prince Edward Island, Canada. He took potatoes

with him, and the community existed on potatoes and cod for many years.

POTATOES TODAY

Today, potatoes are grown in more than 180 countries under a wide range of climatic conditions. Large-scale potato production is big business and is highly mechanized. Row upon row of furrows are made in fields by machines, and mechanical planters drop in the seed potatoes. Computer-aided machines determine the depth and distance between the furrows and the timing of spraying and harvesting the crop.

In the garden, however, potatoes can be grown without the aid of sophisticated, computer-controlled machinery. The enormous range of cultivars that are available means that even in

ABOVE Growing a range of cultivars can give the home grower potatoes almost all year round.

BELOW Potatoes are a valuable source of protein, fibre and vitamin C.

a comparatively small vegetable plot a worthwhile crop can be grown economically and easily, and if a range of cultivars is chosen to give potatoes over a long period, it is possible to have home-grown potatoes almost all year round.

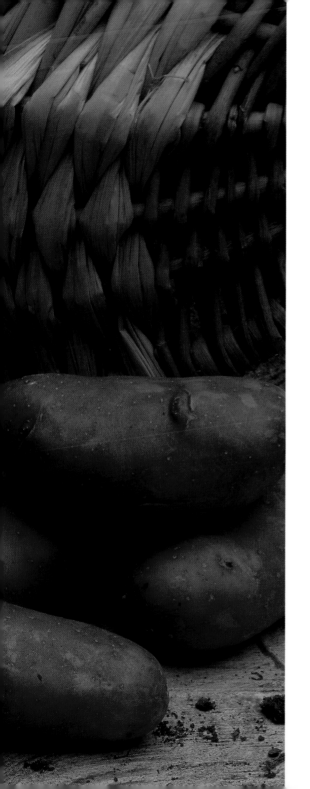

types of
potato

There are literally hundreds of potato cultivars to choose among: small, flaky new potatoes with a sweet, buttery flavour; traditional maincrops with soft, earthy-tasting, floury centres; waxy gold-coloured maincrops with a firm, velvety texture; and small, misshapen speciality potatoes which give a delicious crunch to salads and casseroles. There is also an ever-expanding collection of vivid red, pink, purple and blue potatoes, as well as old-fashioned, so-called heritage cultivars, which are being brought back into cultivation. It is possible to choose a different variety for every potato dish, and if you grow a range of cultivars you can have home-grown crops throughout almost every month of the year.

First early potatoes

Potatoes are classified by the length of time they take to mature, although this can, of course, be affected by the weather and the climate. First earlies, which are also called new potatoes, are planted in early spring for harvesting in early summer.

ACCENT

A uniform oval or round potato, with a light yellow, smooth skin, a waxy flesh that holds its shape, and a bland flavour.
Origin Netherlands, 1994.
Availability Netherlands, United Kingdom.
Suitable cooking and serving methods Boiling and salad.

ALCMARIA

A long, oval potato, with yellow skin, firm flesh and shallow eyes.
Origin Netherlands, 1970.

Availability Italy, United Kingdom.
Suitable cooking and serving methods Baking, boiling and most other methods.

AMINCA

An oval, medium to large potato, with light yellow skin and cream or light yellow flesh, medium deep eyes and a dry texture. Often used for crisp (potato chip) production.
Origin Netherlands, 1977.

'Alcmaria'

'Aminca'

CLEANING

Freshly harvested home-grown potatoes will still have some earth attached to them, and will need some scrubbing before cooking. Giving them a light wash in water will probably be sufficient before boiling them. However, if you are not going to cook your potatoes immediately, avoid scrubbing them with water because they can start to go mouldy in warm or damp weather.

1 If potatoes are dirty, use a small scrubbing brush or a gentle scourer to clean and remove the peel of new potatoes.

2 Carefully remove green or discoloured patches or black eyes with a pointed knife or potato peeler, unless you are going to peel them after cooking, when they will come out of their skins easily. Place the potatoes immediately in enough water to cover them.

'Carlingford'

'Duke of York'

Availability Denmark, Italy, United Kingdom.
Suitable cooking and serving methods Baking, boiling and deep-frying.

CARLINGFORD

A round or oval potato with white skin and flesh, shallow to medium eyes, and a firm and waxy cooked texture. An excellent new or baby potato, it is best not overcooked. It is very good steamed, microwaved and baked in wedges.
Origin Northern Ireland, 1982.
Availability Australia, United Kingdom.

Suitable cooking and serving methods Baking, boiling and deep-frying.

DUKE OF YORK

A long, oval potato with pale whitish-yellow skin, light yellow flesh, a firm cooked texture and a rich, sweet flavour. It is popular for cultivating at home and is best eaten when the potatoes are young.
Alternative name Eersteling.
Origin Scotland, 1891.
Availability Netherlands, France, United Kingdom.
Suitable cooking and serving methods Baking, boiling, roasting and most other methods.

SCRAPING

Really new potatoes peel very easily, often just by rubbing them in your hands. You can tell a good new potato by how easily the skin rubs or flakes off.

Use a small, sharp knife to scrape away the flaky skin and place the potatoes immediately in enough water to cover them.

'Duke of York Red'

PEELING

Much of the goodness and flavour of a potato is in the skin and just below it. You can boil the potatoes, allow them to cool and then peel them. The taste is much fresher and earthier if they are prepared this way and they are perfect for eating plain or simply garnished. Leave the skins on occasionally, which gives more taste and added texture, and is a vital source of fibre in the diet.

To peel potatoes, use a sharp potato peeler to remove the thinnest layer possible in long, even strips. Place the potatoes in a saucepan of water so they are just covered. Cook them immediately to avoid loss of vitamin C.

DUKE OF YORK RED

This is an old variety of potato which has a long, oval shape. Its most distinctive characteristic is the very red skin. However, this colour is mainly lost when the potato is cooked. It has a firm, light yellow flesh and is considered tasty by most gardeners and cooks.
Alternative name Rode Eersteling.
Origin Netherlands, 1842.
Availability Netherlands, United Kingdom (but quite rare).
Suitable cooking and serving methods Boiling and salad.

EPICURE

A round potato with a white skin and creamy white flesh. It has a firm texture, deep eyes and a distinctive flavour. The traditional Ayrshire potato, it is popular and easy to grow, and is still grown in Scottish gardens.
Origin United Kingdom, 1897.
Availability Canada, United Kingdom.

Suitable cooking and serving methods Baking and boiling.

'Epicure'

'Irish Cobbler'

IRISH COBBLER

A round, white, medium to large potato with a smooth creamy white skin and flesh. It was widely grown in the United Kingdom at the turn of the 20th century, probably because it matures earlier than other varieties, but it has mainly been grown in the USA. It bruises easily.

Alternative name America.

Origin USA, 1876.

Availability Canada, South Korea, USA.

Suitable cooking and serving methods Boiling, deep-frying, mashing and most other methods.

PENTLAND JAVELIN

A medium-sized, oval potato, with a white skin, white flesh, and a soft, waxy texture. It is good for home growing and cooks well as a new potato, but also bakes and roasts well later in the season.

Origin Scotland, 1968.

Availability United Kingdom.

Suitable cooking and serving methods Boiling, salad, baking and roasting.

PENTLAND MARBLE

A small, round to oval, white-skinned potato, with light yellow, waxy flesh. The good flavour and

'Pentland Javelin'

CHOPPING

Potatoes are often required to be chopped for recipes such as salads and dishes that include leftovers. If you are cooking them first, the best potatoes to choose are the waxy ones, which stay firm. They chop most easily when they are cold and peeled.

To chop, cut the potato in half, then in half again and again until it is cut up evenly, as small as is required for the dish.

waxy texture make it ideal for salads. It was neglected for some years, and has only recently been reintroduced into the market.

Origin Scotland, 1970.

Availability United Kingdom.

Suitable cooking and serving methods Boiling and salad.

'Pentland Marble'

SLICING

How you slice potatoes will affect both the appearance of the dish and the cooking time. Cut slices the same thickness to cook evenly. To make rounder slices, cut across the width of the potato; for longer slices cut along the length. If you need to slice cooked potatoes for a recipe, undercook them slightly so they don't fall to pieces, and let them get cold before handling. For most toppings, cut them about 3mm/⅛in thick.

Put the tip of the knife on the work surface or board first, then press the heel of the knife down firmly to create nice even slices.

PREMIERE

A large, oval potato with a light yellow skin, firm yellow flesh and a good flavour. It is not as waxy as many other early potatoes.
Origin Netherlands, 1979.
Availability Bulgaria, Canada, Netherlands, United Kingdom.
Suitable cooking and serving methods Baking, boiling, deep-frying and roasting.

ROCKET

A uniformly round, white-skinned potato with white flesh, a firm, waxy texture and a good flavour. This is one of the earliest potatoes of the new season.
Origin United Kingdom, 1987.
Availability New Zealand, United Kingdom.
Suitable cooking and serving methods Baking, boiling, deep-frying, mashing, roasting and salad.

ULSTER PRINCE

A large, kidney-shaped potato with white skin and white flesh. It is best eaten early in the season.
Origin United Kingdom, 1947.
Availability Irish Republic, United Kingdom (very rare).
Suitable cooking and serving methods Baking, boiling, deep-frying and roasting.

ULSTER SCEPTRE

A smallish oval potato with yellow-white skin and creamy, waxy, firm flesh. Sometimes blackening can occur after cooking.
Origin Northern Ireland, 1963.
Availability Northern Ireland.
Suitable cooking and serving methods Boiling, roasting and salad.

VANESSA

A long, oval potato with pink to red skin and a light yellow flesh.
Origin Netherlands, 1973.
Availability Netherlands, United Kingdom.
Suitable cooking and serving methods Boiling, roasting and salad.

WHITE ROSE

A large, very long and flat potato with a smooth white skin, bright white flesh and quite deep eyes.
Alternative names American Giant, Wisconsin Pride, California Long White.
Origin USA, 1893.
Availability Canada, USA.
Suitable cooking and serving methods Baking, boiling and mashing.

'Premiere'

'Rocket'

'Ulster Prince' (top), 'Ulster Sceptre'

Potatoes can be grated before or after cooking, depending on how you will be using them. They are easier to grate after cooking, when they have had time to cool, and can be grated on a large blade straight into the cooking dish or frying pan. Don't overcook the potatoes as they will just fall to pieces. Floury potatoes are ideal for mashing, and waxy ones for making rösti or hash.

Raw potatoes exude a surprising amount of starchy liquid that is vital to helping some dishes stick together. Check before you start whether you need to keep this liquid. The recipe should also tell you whether to rinse off the starchy liquid or just dry the potatoes on kitchen paper.

WINSTON

A relatively new variety of potato. A noticeable characteristic is that it has almost no eyes, making a smooth, easy-to-peel skin. It is an oval potato with a white skin and a very firm texture. This potato makes a very good early-season baker.

Origin Scotland, 1992.

Availability New Zealand, United Kingdom.

Suitable cooking and serving methods Baking, deep-frying, roasting and salad.

'Winston'

Second early potatoes

These are still "new" potatoes but are planted in late spring and are harvested, after 15 to 18 weeks, from mid- to late summer.

'Alex'

SLICING WITH A MANDOLINE

Named after the musical instrument, the mandoline has several different cutting blades, which vary both the size and shape of the cut potato. The blades are fitted into a metal, plastic or wooden framework for ease of use. It is excellent for slicing potatoes evenly, and can produce slices from very thin to very thick, as well as fluted slices for crinkle-cut style crisps (potato chips). It's quite a dangerous gadget and needs handling with respect because of its very sharp blades.

Fix the blade to the thickness required, then, holding the potato, carefully slide it firmly up and down or across the blade. Take care when the potato gets smaller, as it's easy to cut one's fingers.

ALEX

This long, oval potato has a creamy, waxy texture and good, mild flavour. There is a splash of blue on the skin.

Origin Denmark, 1995.
Availability Europe, United Kingdom.
Suitable cooking and serving methods Salad and most other methods.

ANYA

A small finger potato with a knobbly, long oval shape and a pale, pink-beige skin, white flesh, a waxy texture and a pleasant nutty flavour.
Origin Scotland, 1997.
Availability United Kingdom.

Suitable cooking and serving methods Boiling and salad.

AUSONIA

An oval potato with a white skin and a light yellow, mealy flesh. It is susceptible to discolouring after cooking. It is predominantly sold in various pre-packed forms. It was developed from the popular 'Wilja'.
Origin Netherlands, 1981.
Availability Greece, Netherlands, United Kingdom.
Suitable cooking and serving methods Baking, boiling and most other methods.

'Anya'

'British Queen'

BRITISH QUEEN

A kidney-shaped potato with a smooth, white skin and a very white, floury flesh. It is best cooked with the skins left on to retain the excellent flavour. It was a very popular variety at the turn of the 20th century, and is enjoying a revival.

Origin Scotland, 1894.
Availability United Kingdom.
Suitable cooking and serving methods Baking, boiling, roasting, processing and salad.

BF15

A long, slightly bent potato with a smooth, yellow skin and yellow flesh that is firm and waxy with a very good flavour. It was derived from the maincrop 'Belle de Fontenay' but is slightly earlier.

Origin France, 1947.
Availability France.
Suitable cooking and serving methods Boiling and salad.

CATRIONA AND BLUE CATRIONA

A large, kidney-shaped potato with skin that has beautiful purple splashes around the eyes, pale yellow flesh and a very good flavour.

Origin Scotland, 1920; Blue Catriona, United Kingdom, 1979.
Availability United Kingdom.
Suitable cooking and serving methods Baking, boiling and most other methods.

'Catriona'

DICING

If the recipe calls for diced potatoes, this means you have to be more precise than for chopping and cut the potato into evenly shaped cubes. This is usually so that all the sides brown neatly or the pieces cook through evenly.

To make dice, trim the sides and ends of the potato to make a neat rectangle first (keeping the outside pieces for mash or for adding to a soup). Then cut the rectangle into thick, even slices. Turn over the stack of slices and cut them lengthways into thick batons and finally crossways into even cubes that are the size needed for the recipe you are following.

'BF15'

MAKING CRISPS

Home-made crisps (potato chips) can be very fiddly if you do not have the right tools for making them. To make a large batch slice the potatoes in a food processor, but for a small batch the slicing blade on a standard grater should give thin enough potato slices if you use it carefully. It is possible to use a sharp knife to make crisps, but you need to be very careful to cut fine slices.

EDZELL BLUE

A round, blue-skinned potato with bright white flesh, which is floury and tasty. Boil with care as it falls apart easily. It is very good steamed and in microwave recipes.
Origin Scotland, pre-1915.
Availability Scotland.
Suitable cooking and serving methods Boiling and mashing.

ESTIMA

A uniform oval shape, this potato has shallow eyes, a light yellow skin and flesh, a firm, moist texture and a mild flavour. It is the most widely grown second early and has an exceptionally long season. It makes a particularly good baking potato early in the year and it was one of the first to destroy the myth that yellow potatoes could not be popular.
Origin Netherlands, 1973.
Availability Algeria, Northern Europe.
Suitable cooking and serving methods Baking, boiling, deep-frying, roasting and most other methods.

KEPPLESTONE KIDNEY

A blue-skinned, classically shaped potato with yellow flesh and a rich buttery taste.
Origin United Kingdom, 1919.
Availability United Kingdom.
Suitable cooking and serving methods Boiling.

'Edzell Blue'

'Estima'

'Kepplestone Kidney'

LINZER DELIKATESS

A small, oval- to pear-shaped potato with a pale yellow skin, yellow flesh and a firm and waxy texture. The flavour is similar to the early maincrop La Ratte, although not so distinctive. It makes a good salad potato.
Origin Austria, 1976.
Availability Austria, United Kingdom
Suitable cooking and serving methods Boiling and salad.

MARFONA

A round- to oval-shaped potato with light beige to yellow skin and flesh, a smooth, waxy texture and a slightly sharp taste.
Origin Netherlands, 1975.

Availability Cyprus, Greece, Israel, Netherlands, Portugal, Turkey, United Kingdom.
Suitable cooking and serving methods Baking, boiling, deep-frying, mashing and most other methods.

MARIS PEER

A round- to oval-shaped potato with a cream skin and flesh, shallow to medium eyes and a firm cooked texture. Best when young as new potatoes, as they will not break up on cooking. The larger, later season ones bake well either whole or in wedges.
Origin United Kingdom, 1962.
Availability United Kingdom.
Suitable cooking and serving methods Boiling, deep-frying and salad.

'Marfona'

CHIPS

The French give their chips (French fries) various names, depending on how thin or thick they are cut. The larger you cut them the healthier they will be, since they will absorb less fat during the cooking. You can also make chips with their skins on, giving additional fibre.

Traditional chips
Use the largest suitable potatoes and cut the potatoes into 1.5cm/⅝in thick slices, or thicker if you wish. Turn the slices on their side and cut into 1.5cm/⅝in batons, or thicker or thinner if you prefer.

Pommes frites
Cut as for chips but slice again into neat, even batons about 6mm/⅓in thick, either by hand or with a machine.

Pommes allumettes
Cut the potato into a neat rectangle by removing the rounded sides, then into thin slices and then julienne strips. Pommes allumettes should be about half the thickness of pommes frites.

MAKING RIBBONS

Thin ribbons, which are delicious when deep-fried, can be simply cut with a potato peeler.

Peel the potato like an apple, to give long strips. Keep the ribbons in a bowl of cold water.

'Norchip'

Suitable cooking and serving methods Baking, boiling, deep-frying, mashing and roasting.

NADINE

A potato with a creamy yellow skin and white flesh, a firm, waxy texture but a slightly disappointing taste. It is sometimes available as small new potatoes with soft young skins, which scrub easily. The larger ones are good baked and in wedges.
Origin Scotland, 1987.
Availability Australia, Canary Isles, New Zealand, Spain, United Kingdom.

Suitable cooking and serving methods Baking, boiling, mashing and salad.

NORCHIP

A round to oblong potato with a smooth white skin and white flesh. It is excellent for deep-frying.
Origin North Dakota, 1968.
Availability Canada, USA (North Carolina, Dakota).
Suitable cooking and serving methods Baking, boiling and deep-frying.

MONA LISA

A long, oval potato, sometimes kidney-shaped, with yellow skin and flesh that is waxy but becomes floury when cooked. It has a good nutty flavour. It grows quite large for a new potato and is surprisingly versatile in cooking.
Origin Netherlands, 1982.
Availability France, Greece, Netherlands, Portugal.

'Mona Lisa'

'Nadine'

ROSEVAL

This older potato is as popular for its appearance as it is for its taste. An oval potato with dark red, almost purple skin and golden-yellow flesh, it has a waxy texture and a deliciously buttery flavour. It is a very distinctive-looking potato, which proved a great success when cooked in a microwave.

Origin France, 1950.

Availability Australia, France, Israel, New Zealand, United Kingdom.

Suitable cooking and serving methods Boiling and salad.

SAXON

This potato has a white skin and white flesh, a firm, moist texture and excellent flavour. It is a new general purpose potato, which is still finding its niche, but it is very popular in the pre-packed potato market.

'Roseval'

Origin United Kingdom, 1992.

Availability United Kingdom (still rare).

Suitable cooking and serving methods Baking, boiling and deep-frying.

'Saxon'

HASSELBACK AND FAN POTATOES

Children often refer to these as hedgehogs as they look quite spiky when roasted to a crispy, golden brown. Peel and dry the potatoes, then slice, brush with oil and put them to roast as soon as possible, before they begin to discolour.

To make hasselback potatoes, cut large potatoes in half and place cut side down on a board. With a sharp knife, cut very thin slices across the potato from end to end, slicing deep but not quite through the potato.

To make potato fans, use medium potatoes of long or oval shape and cut them at a slight angle, slicing almost but not quite all the way through. Press the potato gently on the top until it flattens and fans out at the same time. If you don't cut far enough through it will not fan, but if you cut too far it will split into sections. The best way to cook both these potatoes is to coat them with melted butter and oil and roast them in the oven, preheated to 190°C/375°F/ Gas 5, for 40–50 minutes.

'Shetland Black'

BLANCHING

Potatoes are blanched (part-cooked) to soften the skin for easy peeling, to remove excess starch for certain recipes and to par-cook before roasting. Use a draining spoon or basket to remove large chunks of potato, but when you are cooking small pieces put them in a wire basket for easy removal.

Place the prepared potatoes in a pan of cold water. Bring slowly to the boil and boil gently for 2–5 minutes, depending on their size. Drain and use or leave in the cooling water until required.

SHETLAND BLACK

This potato has an inky blue-black skin with yellow flesh and a unique purple ring inside. It is very fluffy and floury with an exceptionally sweet, buttery flavour. An attractive potato that, if handled carefully, can be great in salads or served simply with butter. It is also good mashed, but the flesh goes slightly grey-blue.

Alternative name Black Kidney.
Origin United Kingdom, 1923.
Availability United Kingdom.
Suitable cooking and serving methods Boiling and mashing.

SPUNTA

This curiously named potato has become popular throughout the world since its introduction. It is a medium-large, long potato, often kidney- or pear-shaped, with a light yellow skin and golden flesh.

Origin Netherlands, 1968.
Availability Argentina, Australia, Cyprus, Greece, Indonesia, Italy, Malaysia, Mauritius, Netherlands, New Zealand, Portugal, Thailand, Tunisia, United Kingdom, Vietnam.
Suitable cooking and serving methods Baking, boiling, deep-frying, mashing, roasting, salad and most other methods.

'Spunta'

'Wilja'

WILJA

A long, oval potato with a pale yellow skin and flesh, which is quite firm and has a slightly dry texture. One of the most widely grown of the second-early potatoes, it is often available in the maincrop season.

Origin Netherlands, 1967.
Availability Netherlands, Pakistan.
Suitable cooking and serving methods Boiling, deep-frying, mashing and roasting.

YUKON GOLD

A large, oval to round potato with buff-coloured skin, yellow flesh, pink eyes and a slightly mealy texture. It is an excellent baking potato with a delicious flavour, which is very popular in the international speciality market. This was the first successful North American yellow-fleshed potato.

Origin Ontario, Canada, 1980.
Availability Canada, USA (California, Michigan).
Suitable cooking and serving methods Baking, boiling and deep-frying.

'Yukon Gold'

STEAMING

All potatoes steam well, but this gentle way of cooking is particularly good for very floury potatoes and those that fall apart easily. Small potatoes, such as new potatoes, taste really delicious when they are steamed in their skins. Make sure that larger potatoes are cut quite small, in even-size chunks or thick slices. Leaving cooked potatoes over a steaming pan of water is also a good way to keep them warm.

1 Place the prepared potatoes in a sieve, colander or vegetable steamer over a deep pan of boiling, salted water. Cover as tightly as possible and steam for 5–7 minutes if they are sliced or cut small, increasing the time to 20 minutes or more if the potatoes are in quite large pieces.

2 Towards the end of the cooking time, test a few of the potatoes with a sharp knife. If they are cooked, turn off the heat and leave until you are ready to serve them. They will keep warm above the water.

Maincrop potatoes

These potatoes are planted in spring but are not harvested for at least 18 to 22 weeks, in late summer to early autumn. Maincrop potatoes go into long-term storage for sale in the next season, unlike earlies, which go straight into the shops. The following potatoes crop throughout the maincrop season.

AILSA

A round or oval, medium-sized potato, with a white skin and light, creamy-coloured flesh. It has a pleasant flavour and a floury texture.
Origin Scotland, 1984.
Availability United Kingdom.
Suitable cooking and serving methods Boiling and deep-frying.

AMBO

A potato with a creamy skin, large pink eye patches and a very white, bland, floury flesh.

'Désirée'

Origin Irish Republic, 1993.
Availability Irish Republic, New Zealand, Switzerland, United Kingdom.
Suitable cooking and serving methods Baking, boiling and most other methods.

DESIREE

An oval potato with shallow eyes and a smooth, red skin, pale creamy yellow flesh, firm texture and a good flavour. It is said to be the world's most popular red-skinned potato, widely grown and sold from farms and markets. It is good roasted, and it holds its shape when boiled briefly, steamed or microwaved.
Origin Netherlands, 1962.
Availability Algeria, Argentina, Australia, Cameroon, Canada, Chile, Iran, Irish Republic, Malawi, Morocco, Netherlands, New Zealand, Pakistan, Portugal, Sri Lanka, Tunisia, Turkey, United Kingdom, USA.
Suitable cooking and serving methods Baking, boiling, deep-frying, mashing, roasting, salad and most other methods.

'Ailsa'

'Ambo'

'Francine'

Boiling is the simplest way of cooking potatoes. Place potatoes of a similar size, either whole or cut into chunks, with or without their skins, in a pan with sufficient water just to cover them. Cover the pan with a tightly fitting lid, then sprinkle on 5–10ml/1–2 tsp salt or to taste, and bring slowly to the boil.

FRANCINE

This is a relatively modern potato with a red skin, white-cream flesh, soft yet waxy texture and an earthy taste. It is great for gratins and for steaming.

Origin France, 1993.

Availability France, Germany, United Kingdom.

Suitable cooking and serving methods Boiling and salad.

KING EDWARD

This oval- to kidney-shaped potato has a white skin with pink coloration, cream to pale yellow flesh and a floury texture.

Origin United Kingdom, 1902; 1916.

Availability Australia, New Zealand, Portugal, Spain, United Kingdom.

Suitable cooking and serving methods Baking, deep-frying, mashing and roasting.

• Floury potatoes need very gentle boiling or you may find the outside is cooked before the inside is ready and they will become mushy or fall apart in the pan.

• New potatoes, which have a higher vitamin C content, should be put straight into boiling water and cooked for about 15 minutes and not left soaking.

• Very firm salad potatoes can be put into boiling water, simmered for 5–10 minutes and then left to stand in the hot water for another 10 minutes until required.

• When they have finished cooking, drain through a colander and then return them to the pan to dry off, as wet or soggy potatoes are not very appetizing. For really dry, peeled potatoes (for mashing for instance), leave them over a very low heat so any moisture can escape. If you like, you can sprinkle the potatoes with salt and shake occasionally until the potatoes stick to the sides of the pan.

• If wished, wrap the potatoes in a clean dish towel until ready to serve dry and fluffy.

'King Edward'

'Pentland Crown'

PENTLAND CROWN

An oval to round potato with a white skin and creamy white flesh. The first of a number of Pentland cultivars to become popular in the 1970s, especially in eastern England, it is rather out of favour now as it does not cook as well as other varieties.

Origin Scotland, 1959.
Availability United Kingdom (Scotland), Malawi.
Suitable cooking and serving methods Baking, boiling and roasting.

PIKE

A medium, round potato with quite deep eyes, buff-coloured, slightly netted skin and creamy flesh. It has a tendency to discolour after it has been cooked.

Origin Pennsylvania, 1996.
Availability Canada, USA.
Suitable cooking and serving methods Baking, boiling and deep-frying.

REMARKA

A large, oval potato with a creamy white skin, pale yellow flesh and a good flavour. This potato is ideal for organic gardening as it is a very disease-resistant form. It makes a particularly good baking potato.

Origin Netherlands, 1992.
Availability Netherlands, Portugal, Spain, United Kingdom.
Suitable cooking and serving methods Baking, boiling, deep-frying and roasting.

'Remarka'

POTATO PARCELS

Baked potatoes wrapped in foil make a simple and delicious dish. If you leave the potatoes in their skins you could prepare them well in advance and put them to cook in an automatic oven for when you get home.

Wash or scrub and dry small potatoes, then wrap them up in a parcel with several knobs of butter, a sprinkle of seasoning and a sprig or two of mint, tarragon or chives. Bake at 190°C/375°F/ Gas 5 for about 40–50 minutes for 450g/lb potatoes.

RED RASCAL

A red-skinned, yellow-fleshed potato, with a slightly floury texture and a good flavour.

Origin Unknown.
Availability New Zealand.
Suitable cooking and serving methods Baking, mashing and roasting.

SNOWDEN

A round, slightly flat potato with mildly netted, light tan skin and creamy flesh. Used in Canada for chip (French fry) processing.

Origin USA, 1990.
Availability Canada, USA.
Suitable cooking and serving methods Baking, boiling and deep-frying.

Early maincrop potatoes

Maincrop potatoes will be ready to harvest after 18–22 weeks, but some tend to crop earlier than others. The potatoes in this section will, in average conditions, crop after about 18 weeks.

ATLANTIC

An oval to round potato with light, scaly, buff skin and white flesh. It is used largely for chips (French fries).
Origin USA, 1978.
Availability Australia, Canada, New Zealand, USA (North Carolina).
Suitable cooking and serving methods Baking, boiling, deep-frying, mashing and roasting.

AVALANCHE

A round or oval, medium-sized potato, with a white skin, firm, creamy flesh and good, slightly sweet flavour.
Origin Northern Ireland, 1989.
Availability United Kingdom (still rare).
Suitable cooking and serving methods Boiling and mashing.

'Bintje'

BINTJE

A long, oval potato with a pale yellow skin, starchy flesh and a really distinctive flavour.
Origin Netherlands, 1910.
Availability Australia, Brazil, Canada, Denmark, Finland, Italy, Netherlands, New Zealand, Sweden, Thailand, United Kingdom.
Suitable cooking and serving methods Baking, boiling, deep-frying, roasting and salad.

'Atlantic'

'Avalanche'

SHALLOW FRYING

This is a quick way to use up leftover potatoes. Use a heavy-based, large frying pan to allow an even distribution of heat and to give sufficient room to turn the food as it cooks.

1 Heat together about 25g/1oz/ 2 tbsp butter and 30ml/2 tbsp oil until bubbling. Put an even layer of cooked or par-cooked potatoes in the hot fat, taking care not to splash yourself. Leave for 4–5 minutes until the undersides turn golden-brown.

2 Turn over the potatoes gently with a large fish slice once or twice during cooking until they are golden-brown all over.

'Cara White'

CARA WHITE AND RED

A round or oval potato, with a white skin and pink eyes, cream flesh, mild flavour and moist, waxy texture. The pink-skinned variety also has creamy flesh. They are good for cultivating at home, but do not grow well in very wet soil.
Origin Irish Republic, 1976.
Availability Cyprus, Egypt, Irish Republic, Israel, United Kingdom.
Suitable cooking and serving methods Baking, boiling, deep-frying and all other methods.

DEEP-FRYING

When deep-frying potatoes, whether you use oil or solid fat, be sure it is fresh and clean. The chips (French fries) must be well dried as water can cause the fat to bubble up dangerously. Always fry in small batches so that the temperature does not drop too much when you add the food and it can cook and brown evenly. Remove any burned pieces after each batch as this can taint the fat.

• To deep-fry chips, fill a chip pan, a deep heavy saucepan with tight-fitting lid or a deep-fat fryer, about half full with clean fat. Heat to 160°/325°F for blanching, or 190°/375°F for second cooking or for crisps (potato chips). A piece of bread, dropped in the oil, should turn golden in about one minute.

• When making chips they are best blanched first in hot fat to cook through and seal them without browning. These can then be removed, drained and frozen when cool. Give them a final cooking when you are almost ready to eat, to crisp them up and turn them golden-brown.

• Before frying, dry the chips very thoroughly in a cloth or on kitchen paper. Any moisture will make the fat splash and spit. Heat the basket in the fat first, then add the chips to the basket (don't overfill or they will not cook evenly) and lower slowly into the pan. If the fat appears to bubble up too much remove the basket and cool the fat slightly.

• Shake the pan of chips occasionally to allow even cooking, and cook until they are crisp and golden. Remove with a draining spoon or wire basket and drain well against the side of the pan first.

• Tip the chips on to kitchen paper to get rid of the excess fat before serving, sprinkled with salt.

'Claret'

'Fianna'

CLARET

A smooth rosy red-skinned potato, with a round to oval shape and cream, firm flesh.
Origin Scotland, 1996.
Availability Scotland.
Suitable cooking and serving methods Good all-round potato.

FIANNA

A round to oval potato with a smooth, white skin, firm flesh and a pleasant, floury texture.
Origin Netherlands, 1987.

'Forty Fold', white and russet

'Maris Piper'

Availability Netherlands, New Zealand, United Kingdom.
Suitable cooking and serving methods Baking, deep-frying, mashing and roasting.

FORTY FOLD, WHITE AND RUSSET

The irregularly-shaped tubers have deep eyes, white or vivid purple skin splashed with white or russet, creamy flesh and a good flavour. This potato was a popular Victorian speciality, which is currently enjoying a revival, as are many of the older varieties.
Origin United Kingdom, 1893; Russet, United Kingdom, 1919.
Availability United Kingdom (quite rare).
Suitable cooking and serving methods Baking, boiling and most other methods.

MARIS PIPER

An oval potato with a cream skin and flesh and a pleasant floury texture and taste. One of the most popular potatoes in Britain, especially for fish and chips.
Origin United Kingdom, 1964.
Availability Portugal, United Kingdom.
Suitable cooking and serving methods Baking, deep-frying and roasting.

MONDIAL

This less common variety of potato has a long, oval profile with a yellow skin and flesh and a slightly mealy texture.
Origin Netherlands, 1987.
Availability Greece, Israel, Netherlands, New Zealand.
Suitable cooking and serving methods Baking, deep-frying, mashing and roasting.

'Mondial'

NICOLA

A medium to long oval potato with a smooth, yellow skin and deep yellow flesh. The texture is waxy with an excellent buttery taste. At one time mainly grown in Mediterranean countries, this salad-style potato has become so popular that it is being grown much more widely. It is ideal for all-round use as well as being particularly good as a salad potato.

Origin West Germany, 1973.

Availability Australia, Austria, Cyprus, Egypt, France, Germany, Israel, Morocco, New Zealand, Portugal, Switzerland, Tunisia, United Kingdom.

Suitable cooking and serving methods Baking, boiling, deep-frying, mashing, roasting, salad and most other methods.

'Nicola'

ROASTING

Melt-in-the-mouth crispy-skinned roasties are what Sundays were meant for, so here are some pointers to make sure you get them right every time.

For soft, fluffy-centred roast potatoes, you need to use large baking potatoes – 'Wilja', 'Maris Piper', 'Record', 'Désirée' and 'Kerr's Pink' all give excellent results. Peel and cut into even-size pieces. (You can roast potatoes in their skins but you won't get the crunchy result most people love.) Blanch for 5 minutes, then leave in the cooling water for a further 5 minutes to par-cook evenly. Drain well and return to the pan to dry off completely. Well-drained potatoes with roughened surfaces produce the crispiest results.

A successful roast potato also depends on the fat you cook them in and the temperature. Beef dripping gives the best flavour, although goose fat, if you are lucky enough to find some, is delicious and gives a very light, crisp result. With other roasts you can use lard or, where possible, drain off enough dripping from the joint. A vegetarian alternative is a light olive oil, or olive and sunflower oils mixed.

The fat must be hot enough to seal the potato surfaces immediately. Use a large roasting pan so that you have room to turn the potatoes at least once.

1 Peel the potatoes and cut them into even-size pieces. Blanch the peeled chunks of potato and drain, then shake in the pan or fork over the surfaces to roughen them up.

2 Pour a shallow layer of your chosen fat into a good heavy roasting pan and place it in the oven, heating it to a temperature of 220°C/425°F/Gas 7. Add the dry, forked potatoes and toss immediately in the hot fat.

3 Return to the top shelf of the oven and roast for up to one hour. Once or twice during cooking, remove the roasting pan from the oven and, using a spatula, turn the potatoes over to evenly coat them in fat.

'Pentland Hawk'

'Pentland Squire'

'Picasso'

PENTLAND HAWK

An oval potato with a white skin, creamy flesh and a good flavour. It is very popular in Scotland as it is a good all-round potato which cooks well. It is an excellent keeper, but has a slight tendency to discolour after cooking. It is at its best late in the season.

Origin Scotland, 1966.
Availability United Kingdom.
Suitable cooking and serving methods Baking, boiling, deep-frying and roasting.

PENTLAND SQUIRE

Another of the famous Pentland series, this is an oval potato with a white skin and creamy white flesh, very floury texture and a good flavour. It is a very good baker and is also popular in fish and chip shops in the United Kingdom.

Origin Scotland, 1970.
Availability United Kingdom.
Suitable cooking and serving methods Baking, mashing and roasting.

PICASSO

A small, oval to round potato with quite deep red eyes, a pale skin and white waxy flesh. It is popular in warmer countries.

Origin Netherlands, 1992.
Availability Balearic Islands, Cyprus, Egypt, Netherlands, Portugal, Russia, Spain, United Kingdom.
Suitable cooking and serving methods Boiling and salad.

LA RATTE

A long, tubular, almost banana-shaped potato. It has a brown-yellow skin and creamy flesh, which is firm and waxy with a delicious nutty flavour. It is very popular in France and is growing in popularity elsewhere.

Alternative names Cornichon, Asparges or Princess.
Origin France, 1872.
Availability Australia, Denmark, France, Germany, United Kingdom.
Suitable cooking and serving methods Boiling and salad.

'La Ratte'

'Record'

'Red Rooster'

RECORD

A potato with a white, pink-tinged skin. It has light yellow flesh, a mealy texture and a great flavour.

It is a versatile potato, often sold by the sack in farm shops.

Origin Netherlands, 1932.

Availability Greece, Holland, United Kingdom, Yugoslavia.

Suitable cooking and serving methods Baking, deep-frying, mashing and roasting.

RED PONTIAC

A round to oval potato with dark red, sometimes netted skin, quite deep eyes and white, waxy flesh. Popular around the world, it is good for use in microwave cooking.

Alternative name Dakota Chief.

Origin USA, 1983.

Availability Algeria, Australia, Canada, Philippines, Uruguay, USA (south-eastern states), Venezuela.

Suitable cooking and serving methods Baking, boiling, mashing, roasting and salads.

RED ROOSTER

A flattish, oval potato with bright red skin and firm, buttery, yellow, mild-tasting flesh.

Origin Irish Republic, 1993.

Availability Irish Republic.

Suitable cooking and serving methods Baking, boiling, deep-frying, roasting and salad.

ROMANO

A round to oval potato with a red skin, creamy flesh, a soft, dry texture and a pleasant, mild, nutty taste. It has a lovely colour, which tends to pale during cooking to a soft, rusty beige.

Origin Netherlands, 1978.

Availability Balearic Islands, Cameroon, Russia, Hungary, Netherlands, Portugal, Spain, United Kingdom.

Suitable cooking and serving methods Baking, boiling, mashing, roasting and most other methods.

'Romano'

'Red Pontiac'

BAKING

One of the most comforting and economical meals is a salt-crusted potato baked in its skin with a fluffy centre that is golden with melted butter and cheese, or maybe tuna and mayonnaise.

Allow a 275–350g/10–12oz potato for a good size portion and choose the ones recommended for baking, such as 'Marfona', 'Maris Piper', 'Cara' or 'King Edward'. Cook in the middle of a hot

oven at 220°C/425°F/Gas 7 for 1–1½ hours for very large potatoes or 40–60 minutes for medium potatoes. To test that they are cooked, squeeze the sides to make sure that they are soft.

1 Wash and dry baking potatoes thoroughly, then rub with good oil and add a generous sprinkling of salt. Cook on a baking tray as above. To speed up cooking time and to ensure even cooking throughout, cook the baking potatoes on skewers, or on special potato baking racks.

2 When really tender, cut a cross in the top of each potato and set the tray aside to cool slightly.

3 Hold each hot potato in a clean cloth and squeeze gently from underneath to open up.

4 Place the open potatoes on individual serving plates and put a lump of butter in each one. For a quick topping, add a little grated hard cheese, or a dollop of sour cream and some chopped fresh herbs, such as chives or parsley. Season well.

SANTE

An oval or round potato with white or light yellow skin and flesh and a dry firm texture. This has become the most successful organic potato and is often sold young as a new potato, too.

Origin Netherlands, 1983.
Availability Bulgaria, Canada, Netherlands, United Kingdom.
Suitable cooking and serving methods Boiling, deep-frying and roasting.

SHEPODY

A long, oval potato with white, slightly netted skin, light creamy yellow flesh and a dry, starchy texture. Developed for the chip (French fry) processing market in the USA and seldom found in supermarkets.

Origin Canada, 1980.
Availability Canada, New Zealand, USA (northern states).
Suitable cooking and serving methods Baking, boiling, deep-frying and mashing.

'Sante'

'Shepody'

Late maincrop potatoes

Most maincrop potatoes will be ready to harvest after 18–22 weeks, but some tend to crop later than others. The potatoes in this section will, in average conditions, crop after about 22 weeks.

ARRAN VICTORY

An oval potato with a deep purple skin and bright white flesh. This is the oldest Arran cultivar and is still available. It is a very tasty potato with a floury texture, and although not easy to find it is having a revival of interest.

Alternative name Irish Blues.
Origin Scotland, 1918.
Availability United Kingdom (now rare in England and limited in Scotland and Northern Ireland).
Suitable cooking and serving methods Baking, boiling, roasting and other methods.

BARNA

A uniform, oval, red-skinned potato with a white, slightly waxy flesh and a warm nutty flavour.
Origin Irish Republic, 1993.
Availability Irish Republic, United Kingdom.
Suitable cooking and serving methods Boiling and roasting.

THE BISHOP

A long, oval potato with a white skin and yellow, nutty-flavoured flesh. It is an older variety that has fortunately continued to be available, and has recently become popular once again.
Origin United Kingdom, 1912.
Availability United Kingdom.
Suitable cooking and serving methods Boiling, roasting and salad.

'The Bishop'

CONGO

A striking, small potato with a thin and knobbly shape, very dark, purple-black, shiny skin and beetroot-black flesh. Since it is so small and dark, you might need to do your harvesting on a bright day. The flavour is surprisingly bland and the texture stodgy. It is dry when cooked but retains its colour, making it impressive in

'Arran Victory'

BAKING SKINS

• Bake the potatoes at 220°C/ 425°F/Gas 7 for 1–1½ hours for large potatoes and 40–60 minutes for medium. Cut in half and scoop out the soft centres. (Mash the insides for a supper accompaniment or a pie topping.)
• Brush the skins inside and out with melted butter or a mixture of butter and oil and return to the top of the oven, at the same temperature, for 20 minutes or until the skins are beautifully crisp and golden-brown.

salads and as a garnish. Boil
briefly, steam or microwave,
and peel after
cooking. Congo
potatoes make
good mashed
potatoes or
gnocchi.

Origin Congo.

Availability Australia,
United Kingdom.

**Suitable cooking and serving
methods** Boiling, mashing
and salad.

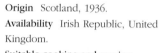

'Congo'

DUNBAR
STANDARD

A long, oval potato with
a white skin and white flesh. It
does particularly well in heavy soil.
This potato has shallow eyes,
making peeling easy. Its full flavour
and firmness suit most forms of
cooking, although it tends to
blacken after cooking.

Origin Scotland, 1936.

Availability Irish Republic, United
Kingdom.

**Suitable cooking and serving
methods** Boiling, roasting and
most other methods.

'Dunbar Standard'

Baking potatoes in the microwave
is a big time-saver. New potatoes
and potato pieces can also be
cooked very quickly and easily.
Always cut or prick the potato
skins first, to prevent bursting. To
bake, allow 4–6 minutes for each
potato, with the setting on high,
increasing by 2–4 minutes for
every additional potato. As a guide
for smaller boiled potatoes, allow
10–12 minutes per 450g/1lb of
cut potatoes on high, or follow
the manufacturer's instructions.

Place large potatoes in a circle on
kitchen paper on the microwave
tray, make cuts around the middle
so the skins don't burst and turn
once during the cooking process.

Place small potatoes in a microwave
bowl with 30–45ml/2–3 tbsp
boiling water. Cover tightly with
microwave film and pierce two or
three times to allow steam to
escape during cooking.

Alternatively, cover the potatoes
with a close-fitting microwave
lid. Leave for 3–5 minutes before
draining, adding a few pieces of
butter, seasoning and a sprig
of mint.

GEMCHIP

A round to oval potato with a smooth, light tan skin and white flesh with the occasional scaly patch. This is a relatively recent variety of potato that is mainly confined to North America
Origin USA, 1989.
Availability Canada, USA (Colorado, Idaho, Oregon, Washington).
Suitable cooking and serving methods Baking, boiling, deep-frying and processing.

'Gemchip'

'Kerr's Pink'

'Pink Fir Apple'

KATAHDIN

A round to oblong potato, with a buff, smooth, thin skin and white, waxy, moist flesh. Until recently, it was mostly popular only in Maine, USA.
Origin USA, 1932.
Availability Canada, New Zealand, USA.
Suitable cooking and serving methods Baking, boiling, salad and most other methods.

KERR'S PINK

A round potato with a pink skin, creamy white flesh and quite deep eyes. It has a mealy, floury texture when cooked.
Origin Scotland, 1917.
Availability Irish Republic, Netherlands, United Kingdom.
Suitable cooking and serving methods Baking, boiling, deep-frying, mashing and roasting.

PINK FIR APPLE

A long, knobbly, misshapen potato with a pink blush on the white skin and creamy yellow flesh. Tubers form clusters of roots under the stem and can be susceptible to blight. It is enjoying something of a revival now but has always been popular with gardeners as it is a good keeper. It is firm and waxy with a delicious, nutty flavour and is best cooked in its skin. The shape makes it impossible to peel until cooked, but it is best cold in salads and tossed in warm dressings or served as new potatoes.
Origin France, 1850.
Availability Australia, France, United Kingdom.
Suitable cooking and serving methods Baking, boiling, roasting and salad.

'Katahdin'

'Up to Date'

SKERRY BLUE

A potato with a rich violet-coloured skin, with deep purple and white mottled or creamy flesh. It has a superb flavour and is highly prized amongst enthusiastic home growers because of its reputation for being blight-resistant.

Origin United Kingdom, c.1846.
Availability United Kingdom.
Suitable cooking and serving methods Boiling.

UP TO DATE

A flattish oval potato with white skin and flesh and a good flavour. It was one of the most popular Victorian varieties.

Origin Scotland, 1894.
Availability Burma, Cyprus, Malawi, Mauritius, Nepal, South Africa, United Kingdom.
Suitable cooking and serving methods Boiling, roasting and most other methods.

'Skerry Blue'

There are a number of different hand mashers available for sale, but the best ones are those that have a strong but open cutting grid that is not too fine.

Simply push down on the cooked potatoes, making sure you cover every area in the pan, and you will get a smooth, yet slightly textured result.

Press potatoes through a ricer for an easy way to prepare light and fluffy mash. For a low-calorie side dish, press the potatoes straight into a heated bowl.

Alternatively, add plenty of butter, some creamy milk and seasoning to taste, then continue mashing the potatoes until you have a creamy, fluffy mixture.

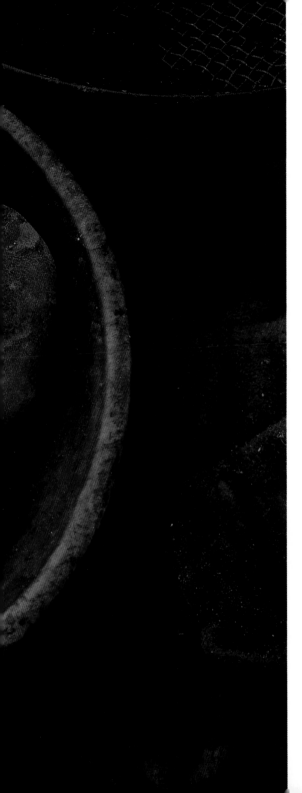

planning and
preparation

Potatoes are best grown in an open, sunny position. Because they are greedy plants, they need fairly rich soil, although they should not be grown on newly manured ground. They also prefer slightly acid conditions. Even though they take up a lot of space in the garden, most gardeners choose to grow at least a few plants because the taste of freshly dug early potatoes is incomparable. As long as you prepare the site carefully and can protect early cultivars from late frosts, you will be rewarded with an easy and reliable crop.

Types of soil

Within reason, potatoes can be grown on almost any type of soil, but it is important to bear in mind that although they are greedy feeders, they should not be planted on newly manured ground. They prefer a soil that is on the acid side of neutral, but whatever your garden soil, you will, with a little work, be able to produce suitable conditions to give a good crop.

CLAY

Most clay soils are fertile, but clay is heavy and the particles cling together, making the soil sticky. Clay soil compacts easily, forming a solid lump that roots find hard to penetrate and that is difficult to dig. Try not to walk on clay soils when they are wet. This tendency to become compacted and sticky means that clay soils are slow to drain, but, once they are drained, they set like concrete. They also tend to be cold and slow to warm up, making them unsuitable for early crops.

Potatoes do not like poor drainage, but if you improve this by adding grit or organic material, or even digging drainage channels if the site is very wet, clay can be ideal, as it is usually rich and often slightly acid.

SANDY SOILS

Soils made up of sand and silts are composed of individual grains that allow the water to pass through quickly. This quick passage of water through the soil tends to

leach (wash) out nutrients, so these soils are often poor. Sandy soil can lead to fungal infections in potatoes, such as scab. But sand also tends to be warmer in winter and is quicker to warm in spring, thus making it easier to grow early crops. Silts contain particles that are more clay-like in texture than those found in sandy soils, and they hold more moisture and nutrients.

Both types of soil are easy to improve and are not difficult to work. Sand does not compact like clay does (although it is still not good practice to walk on beds), but silty soils are susceptible to the impact of feet. Adding organic material can temper their thirst.

LOAM

This is a combination of clay and sandy soils, with the best elements of both. It tends to be free-draining, but at the same time moisture-retentive. This description – free-draining and moisture-retentive – is often used of soils and potting mixes, and it may seem a contradiction. It means that the soil is sufficiently free-draining to allow excess moisture to drain away, but enough moisture is retained for the plant without it standing in stagnant water. Such soils are easy to work at any time of the year, and they warm up well in spring for early crops.

ACID AND ALKALINE SOILS

Another way of classifying soils is by their acidity or alkalinity. Those that are based on peat (peat moss)

are acid; those that include chalk or limestone are alkaline. Gardeners use a scale of pH levels to indicate the degree of acidity or alkalinity. Very acid is 1, neutral is 7 and very alkaline is 14, although soils rarely have values at the extremes of the scale. Although they can be grown on a wider range of soils, potatoes grow best in soils with a pH of 5–6. A test with a soil kit will show the rating in your own garden.

TESTING THE SOIL FOR NUTRIENTS

Collect the soil sample 5–8cm/ 2–3in below the surface. Take a number of samples, but test each one separately. With this kit, mix one part of soil with five parts of water. Shake well in a jar, then allow the water to settle. Draw off some of the settled liquid from the top few centimetres (about an inch) for your test. Carefully transfer the solution to the test chamber in the plastic container, using the pipette. Select a colour-coded capsule (one for each different nutrient). Put the powder in the chamber, replace the cap and shake well. After a few minutes, compare the colour of the liquid with the shade panel of the container.

IMPROVING THE SOIL'S PH

For potatoes, as we have noted, the level to aim at is pH5–6, but anything between 5 and 7 is acceptable. If the soil is too acid, the pH can be adjusted somewhat by adding lime to the soil. Three types of lime can be used for reducing soil acidity. Ordinary lime (calcium carbonate) is the safest to use. Quicklime (calcium oxide) is the strongest and most caustic, but it may cause damage. Slaked lime (calcium hydroxide) is not as strong as quicklime and is therefore less dangerous. Always take safety precautions when applying lime and use the amount recommended by the manufacturer on the packet. Do not add lime at the same time as manure, because this will release ammonia, which can damage the plants. Spread the lime over the soil at the rate prescribed on the packet and rake it in. Do not sow or plant for at least a month.

If the soil is too acid, you can adjust the level, but it is more difficult to make an alkaline soil more acid.

IMPROVING SOIL QUALITY

Perhaps the most important task in any garden is to improve and maintain the quality of the soil. Good quality soil should be the aim of any gardener who wants to grow vegetables or fruit. To ignore the soil is to ignore one of the garden's most important and valuable assets.

The key to improving the soil in your garden is organic material. This is an all-embracing term that

TESTING THE SOIL

Check soil samples 5–8cm/2–3in below the surface. Take a number of samples, and test each one separately. Potatoes grow best in a very rich soil that is fairly acid, around pH5–6.

covers any vegetable matter that has been broken down into an odourless, fibrous compost. It includes such things as rotted garden waste, kitchen vegetable waste, farmyard manures and other plant waste material.

It is important that any such material should be well-rotted. If it is still in the process of breaking down, it will need nitrogen to complete the process and will extract it from the soil. This, of course, is the reverse of what the gardener wants – the gardener's aim is to add nitrogen to the soil. If you are unsure, a good indicator that the material has broken down sufficiently is that it becomes odourless. Even horse manure is free from odour once it has rotted down, and manuring a garden should not be the smelly job it is often depicted as being. Some substances contain undesirable chemicals, but these will be

IMPROVING SOIL FERTILITY

The fertility of the soil is much improved by the addition of organic material, but a quick boost can also be achieved by adding an organic fertilizer, spreading it over the surface and then raking it in.

removed if the material is stacked and allowed to weather. Bark and other shredded woody materials may contain resins, while animal and bird manures may contain ammonia from urea. These chemicals will evaporate or be converted by weathering.

PH VALUES	
1.0	extremely acid
4.0	maximum acidity tolerated by most plants
5.5	maximum acidity for most vegetables
6.0	maximum preferred acidity for most vegetables
6.5	optimum for most vegetables
7.0	neutral, maximum alkalinity for good vegetables
7.5	maximum alkalinity for reasonable vegetables
8.0	maximum tolerated by most plants
14.0	extremely alkaline

Soil conditioners

A wide range of organic soil conditioners are available to the gardener. Some are free – if you do not count the time taken in working and carting them. Others are relatively cheap, and some, usually those bought by the bag, can be quite expensive. However, not everyone has a stable nearby or enough space to store large quantities of material, and many gardeners will therefore need to buy it as required.

FARMYARD MANURE

A traditional material and still much used by many country gardeners, farmyard manure has the advantage of adding bulk to the soil as well as supplying valuable nutrients. The manure can come from any form of livestock, although the most commonly available is horse manure. It can be obtained from most stables, and many are so glad to get rid of it that they will supply it free if you fetch it yourself. There are often stables situated around

the edge of towns, so manure is usually available to town gardeners as well as to those in the country.

Some gardeners do not like the manure when it is mixed with wood shavings rather than with straw, but it is worth bearing in mind that the former is often less likely to contain weed seeds, and as long as it is stacked and allowed to rot down it is excellent for adding to the soil as well as for use as a top-dressing.

All manures should be stacked for a period of at least six months before they are used. When the manure is ready to use, it will have lost its dungy smell.

GARDEN COMPOST

All gardeners should make an effort to recycle as much of their garden and kitchen vegetable waste as possible. In essence, this is simply following nature's pattern, where leaves and stems are formed in the spring and die back in the autumn, falling to the ground and eventually

ABOVE Green manure can be grown as a separate crop or it can be grown between existing crops. It not only fixes nitrogen in the soil, but also provides a good ground cover, keeping the weeds down.

rotting and returning to the plants as nutrients. In the garden some things are removed from the cycle, notably vegetables and fruit, but as much as possible should be returned to the earth.

Compost is not difficult to make, and, of course, it is absolutely free. If you have the space, use several bins at the same time, so there is always some that is ready for use.

Unless weeds that are in seed or diseased plants have been used, compost should be safe to use as a soil conditioner and as a mulch.

LEAF MOULD

This is another natural soil conditioner. It is easy to make and should not cost anything. Only use

ORGANIC MATERIALS

well-rotted farmyard manure

well-rotted garden compost

leaf mould made by yourself; never go down to the local woods and help yourself because this will disturb the wood's own cycle and will impoverish the soil there.

Four stakes knocked into the ground with a piece of wire netting stretched around them will make the perfect container for making leaf mould. Simply add the leaves as they fall from the trees. It will take a couple of years for them to break down and what was a huge heap will shrink to a small layer by the time the process is complete.

Add leaf mould to the soil or use it as a top-dressing. It is usually acid and can be used to reduce the pH of alkaline soil. Pine needles produce a leaf mould that is particularly acid.

PEAT (PEAT MOSS)

This is expensive and does little for the soil because it breaks down too quickly and has little nutritive content. However, the reasons for not using it have nothing to do with its nutritional content. Peat (peat moss) is taken from bogs, rare and fragile ecosystems that are rapidly being depleted. Gardeners do not need to use peat and should always look for environmentally responsible alternatives.

SPENT MUSHROOM COMPOST

Often available locally from mushroom farms, the spent compost is relatively cheap, especially if it is purchased in bulk. It is mainly used in the ornamental part of the garden, but it is still useful in the vegetable garden if it is allowed to rot down. You should allow for the fact that it contains chalk, and so will increase the alkalinity of the soil.

VEGETABLE INDUSTRIAL WASTE

Several industries produce organic waste material that can be useful in the garden. Spent hop waste from the brewing industry is a

GREEN MANURES

Broad (fava) beans: nitrogen fixing
Italian ryegrass: quick growing
Lupins: nitrogen fixing
Mustard: quick growing
Phacelia: quick growing
Red clover: nitrogen fixing
Winter tare: nitrogen fixing

favourite among those who can obtain it. Cocoa shells are now imported, although these are better used as a mulch than as a soil conditioner. They are comparatively high in nitrogen. Several other products are locally available. Allow them to rot well before using.

GREEN MANURE

Some crops can be grown simply to be dug back into the ground, so as to improve the soil condition and to add nutrients. They are useful on light soils that are vacant for any length of time, such as over winter. Green manures can be sown in early autumn and dug in during spring.

WORKING IN ORGANIC MATTER

1 Soil that has been dug in the autumn can have more organic matter worked into the top layer in the spring. Spread the organic matter over the surface.

2 Lightly work the organic material into the top layer of soil with a fork. There is no need for full-scale digging.

Making compost

Compost is a valuable material for any garden, but it is especially useful in the vegetable garden. You can apply compost to a potato plot in spring or summer as a mulch, or dig it into the top 20cm/8in of the soil.

THE PRINCIPLE

The idea behind compost-making is to emulate the process in which a plant takes nutrients from the soil, dies and then rots, putting the nutrients back into the ground. Waste plant material is collected, piled in a heap and left to rot down before being returned to the soil as crumbly, fibrous material.

Because it is in a heap the rotting material generates heat, which encourages it to break down

ABOVE Only a small proportion of the vegetables and flowers for cutting in this plot will be used. This means that most of the foliage and stems can be put in the compost bin.

even more quickly. The heat also helps to kill pests and diseases as well as any seed in the compost. If the mixture is too dry or too wet, the process is slowed down; if there is insufficient air, the heap will go slimy and smell bad.

The process should take about three months, but many gardeners like to retain the heap for longer, growing marrows and courgettes (zucchini) on it before breaking it up for use in the garden.

THE COMPOST BIN

Gardeners always seem to generate more garden waste than they ever thought possible and never have enough compost space, so when planning your bins, make sure you have enough. The aim is to have three: one to hold new waste, one with material that is breaking down and a third that is ready for use.

The bins are often made from wood, and because these can be made to fit the space and amount

of material available, this is still the best option. Sheet materials can also be used. Most ready-made bins are made of plastic, and although these work perfectly well, they may be too small in a busy garden.

The larger the bin, the better it will heat up, but the minimum size is a standard dustbin (trash can). A wooden bin can be made with slats slotted in to form the front wall, so they can be removed to make it easier to take the compost out.

MATERIALS

Most garden plants waste can be used for composting, but avoid perennial weeds, seeding weeds and diseased plants. Woody material, such as hedge clippings, should be shredded. Kitchen

ABOVE A range of organic materials can be used, but avoid cooked kitchen waste, or seeding or perennial weeds. Clockwise from top left: kitchen waste, weeds, shreddings and grass clippings.

vegetable waste, such as peelings and cores, can be used, but avoid cooked vegetables and do not include animal products, which will attract rats and other vermin.

TECHNIQUE

Place a few branches or twiggy material in the bottom of the bin to keep the contents aerated. Put in the material as it becomes available but avoid building up deep layers of any one material, especially grass cuttings. Mix them with other materials. To keep the heap warm, cover it with an old carpet or sheet of plastic. This also prevents excess water from chilling the contents and swamping all the air spaces. The lid should be kept on until the compost is required.

Every so often, add a layer of farmyard manure to provide extra nitrogen to speed things up; or you can buy a compost accelerator. It is not essential to add manure or an accelerator, however – it just means waiting a couple of weeks longer for your compost.

Air is important, and this usually percolates through the side of the bin, so leave a few gaps between the timbers. The colder material around the edges takes longer to break down than that in the centre of the heap, so turn the compost around every so often. This also loosens the pile and allows air to circulate.

MAKING COMPOST

1 A simple compost bin can be made by nailing four flat pallets together. If the bin is roughly made, this will ensure that there will be plenty of air holes between the slats.

2 Pile in the waste, making certain that there are no thick layers of the same material. Grass clippings will not rot down if the layer is too thick because the air cannot penetrate.

3 Keep the compost covered with an old mat or a sheet of plastic to keep in the heat generated by the rotting process and stop the compost from getting too wet in rainy weather.

4 Every so often, turn the compost with a fork to let in air and to move the outside material, which is slow to rot, into the centre to speed up the process. It is easier if you have several bins and turn the compost from one bin into another.

5 When the bin is full, cover the surface with a layer of soil and use it to grow marrows (zucchini), pumpkins or cucumbers. If you want to use the contents as soon as possible, omit the soil and keep covered with polythene.

ABOVE The finished product is dark brown and crumbly and has a sweet, earthy smell, not a rotting one. It can be used straight away or left covered until it is required.

Fertilizers

In nature, when plants die down they return the nutrients they have taken from the soil. In the garden the vegetables are removed and the chain is broken. Compost and other organic materials help to redress the balance, but they may not be able to do the job properly and then fertilizers are needed, applied at regular intervals.

WHAT PLANTS REQUIRE

The main foods required by plants are nitrogen (N), phosphorus (P) and potassium (K), with smaller quantities of magnesium (Mg), calcium (Ca) and sulphur (S). They also require small amounts of trace elements, including iron (Fe) and manganese (Mn). Each of the main nutrients tends to be used by the plant for one specific function.

Each of the main nutrients is used by the plant for one specific function. Nitrogen is used for promoting the rapid growth

ORGANIC FERTILIZERS

blood   bonemeal

seaweed   fish/blood/bone

of the green parts of the plant. Phosphorus, usually in the form of phosphates, is used to create good root growth as well as helping with the ripening of fruits, while potassium, in the form of potash, is used to promote flowering and formation of good fruit.

ORGANIC FERTILIZERS

Concentrated fertilizers are of two types: organic and inorganic. Organic fertilizers consist solely of naturally occurring materials and contain different proportions of nutrients. So bonemeal (ground-up bones), which is strong in phosphates and nitrogen, promotes growth, especially root growth. Bonemeal also has the advantage that it breaks down slowly, gradually releasing the fertilizer over a long period. (Wear gloves when you apply bonemeal.)

Other organic fertilizers include fish, blood and bone (high in nitrogen and phosphates); hoof and horn (nitrogen); and seaweed meal (nitrogen and potash). Because they are derived from natural products without any modification, they are used by organic growers.

INORGANIC FERTILIZERS

These fertilizers have been made artificially, although they are frequently derived from natural rocks and minerals and the process may just involve crushing. They are concentrated and are usually soluble in water, which means that they are instantly available for the

plant. They do. however, tend to wash out of the soil quickly and need to be replaced.

Some are general fertilizers, and might contain equal proportions of nitrogen, phosphorus and potassium, for example. Others are much more specific. Superphosphate, for example, is entirely used for supplying phosphorus, while potassium sulphate is added to the soil if potassium is required.

SLOW-RELEASE FERTILIZERS

A modern trend is to coat the fertilizers so that they are released slowly into the soil. These are expensive in the short term, but because they do not leach away and do not need to be replaced as frequently, they can be considered more economic in the longer term.

They are particularly useful for container planting, where constant watering is necessary which dissolves and washes away normal fertilizer.

INORGANIC FERTILIZERS

Growmore (not   sulphate of
available in USA)   ammonia

potash   superphosphate

Digging the soil

Although some gardeners question its value, winter digging – when there are no crops in the soil – is still an important activity. It breaks up the soil, allowing in water and air, which are important for plant growth. It also allows organic material to be incorporated deep in the soil, right where the roots need it. All weeds and their roots can be removed during digging. It also enables the gardener to spot the more visible types of pest, and destroy any that come to the surface.

1 Divide the space to be dug in half lengthways, marking the area with string. Dividing the plot like this avoids moving excavated soil from one end of the plot to the other.

2 Take out a trench the depth and width of a spade blade. Pile the soil at the end of the other half of the plot, as shown, using a wheelbarrow if necessary.

3 When you remove the next trench, throw the soil forward into the space left by the first. Begin by cutting a slice the width of the bite of soil to be dug.

4 Push the spade in parallel to the trench, taking a slice of soil 15–20cm/6–8in deep. Larger bites may be too heavy to lift comfortably.

5 Loosen the soil by pulling back on the handle, while trying to keep the bite of soil on the spade. Take care that you do not strain your back.

6 Flick the soil over with the wrist, inverting the clod of earth so that the top is buried.

7 When the end of the plot is reached, fill the trench with soil taken from the first row of the return strip.

8 Finally, fill the trench left when digging has been completed with the soil put on one side from the initial excavation.

Garden tools

Looking in the average garden centre, you would imagine that you need a tremendous battery of tools and equipment before you could ever consider gardening, but in fact you can start (and continue) gardening with relatively few.

Tools are personal things, so one gardener may always use a spade for digging, no matter how soft the ground, whereas another would always use a fork as long as the ground was not too heavy. The type of hoe for a particular job is another subject on which gardeners hold widely different opinions.

TYPES OF TOOLS

The main types of tools that are useful for cultivating potatoes are a fork, spade, one or more hoes, and a rake.

A fork is used for general cultivation, lifting potatoes, aerating the soil, and moving and incorporating bulky organic material. A spade is essential for digging, general cultivation and deep weed control.

There are several different types of hoe: cultivator; draw or swan-neck; and push, plate or Dutch. A cultivator is a form of three-pronged hoe that is very good for weeding between rows of potatoes. The tool is drawn between the rows to loosen the earth and with it any seedlings that have just germinated. As their roots are loose in the soil they cannot pick up moisture, so they die.

A draw hoe or swan-neck hoe is pulled towards the gardener in a series of chopping movements. This removes weeds by scraping them off as the hoe is drawn back. In contrast, a push, plate or Dutch hoe is pushed forwards, slicing off the weeds. Hoes are best used in dry weather because they do not open the soil too much, which causes evaporation. In wet weather, however, the cultivator can be useful because it opens the soil and allows the water to drain through.

A rake is essential for breaking up and levelling soil when a vegetable plot is being prepared.

BUYING TOOLS

Most jobs can be done with a small basic kit of tools. When you are buying, always choose the best you can afford. Many cheaper tools are made of pressed steel, which soon becomes blunt, will often bend and may even break. Stainless steel is undoubtedly the best, but tends to be expensive. Ordinary steel implements can be almost as good, especially if you keep them clean. Trowels and hand forks especially are often made of aluminium, but they wear down and blunt quickly and are not good value for money.

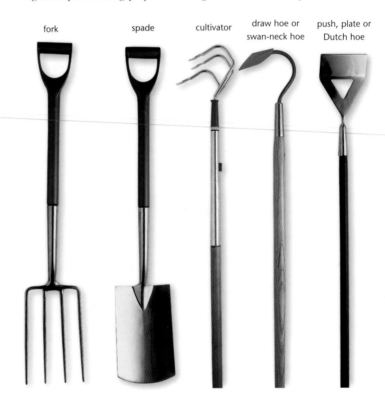

fork   spade   cultivator   draw hoe or swan-neck hoe   push, plate or Dutch hoe

SECOND-HAND

A good way to get a collection of tools is to buy them second-hand, which will be much cheaper than buying new ones. Usually, too, they will be made of better steel than modern ones and still retain a keen edge, even after many years' use. In the past gardening tools were made with a greater variation in design and size. If you go to buy a modern spade, for example, you will probably find that the sizes are all the same – designed for the "average" gardener. Old tools come in all shapes and sizes, and if you find modern tools uncomfortable to use you are more likely to find an old one that suits you.

Not all old tools are good by any means, of course, but by keeping an eye out and buying only good quality ones you will end up with tools that will see you through your gardening career. Car boot sales (garage sales) and rural junk shops (second-hand stores) are the places to look out for them. Avoid antique shops, where such tools are sold at inflated prices to be hung on the wall as decorations rather than to be used for gardening.

CARE AND MAINTENANCE

If you look after your tools they will always be in good working condition and will last a lifetime. Scrape off mud and vegetation as soon as you have used the tools. Once they are clean, run an oily rag lightly over the metal parts. The thin film of oil will stop the metal from corroding. As well as helping the tools to last longer, this also makes them easier to use because less effort is needed to use a clean spade than one with a rough surface of rust.

In addition, keep the wooden parts clean, wiping them over with linseed oil if the wood becomes too dry. Keep all blades sharp. Hang up tools if possible because standing spades and hoes on the ground, especially if it is concrete, will blunt them over time. Keep all tools safely away from children.

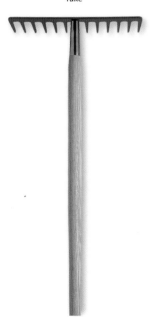

rake

trowel

hand fork

SOIL TESTERS

The chemical composition of the soil can be tested by the gardener by using one of a range of soil testers. The most commonly used checks the acidity/alkalinity of the soil. It is chemical based and involves mixing soil samples with water and checking the colour against a chart. More complicated tests indicate whether there is a shortage of minerals or trace elements. The balance can then be adjusted by adding lime or fertilizers to the soil.

| ACIDITY |
| Alkaline |
| Neutral |
| Acid |
| Very Acid |

soil test meter

gloves

cultivating
potatoes

Potatoes are grown from seed potatoes, which are not seeds in the normal sense of the word but specially grown-on tubers. Seed potatoes are inexpensive, even if you choose to buy organic ones. For every 3m/10ft row you can expect to harvest 9kg/20lb of potatoes, which makes them an economical crop. They are versatile plants, and you can choose to devote part of your vegetable plot to potatoes or to grow just a single first early in a container on your patio. The principle is basically the same wherever you cultivate your potatoes: plant them in 10cm/4in deep holes, draw earth up around them for protection, and harvest your crop when the plants flower.

Chitting and planting

Potatoes are best grown in an open, sunny position. As earlies are likely to emerge through the ground before the last of the frosts, try to choose a warm, protected spot away from any frost pockets. They will grow on most soils, although they prefer slightly acid conditions. The soil should be fertile, but do not plant potatoes on newly manured or limed ground.

CHITTING

Early potatoes should be chitted. This involves standing the seed potatoes on a tray (or in empty egg boxes) so that the eyes are facing upwards. Place the tray in a cool but frost-free place that is in the light, but out of direct sunlight. Short shoots will appear, and this gets the crop off to a good start.

Maincrop potatoes can be treated in the same way, although it is not essential.

PLANTING

First earlies are planted in early spring, followed by second earlies two weeks later. Draw out a row with a hoe about 10cm/4in deep and place the potatoes at 30cm/12in intervals. Rows should be 45cm/18in apart.

Alternatively, the potatoes can be planted in holes dug with a trowel or with a special potato planter. Whichever method you use, cover the potatoes with soil and then draw up more soil to form a low ridge above them.

BELOW When planting potatoes, lay the tubers about 30–45cm/12–18in apart.

When the shoots reach a height of 23–25cm/9–10in, draw earth up around them along the rows to make certain that all the tubers are well covered; otherwise they will turn green. Continue to do this until the foliage of the plants touches across the rows.

Second earlies and maincrop are treated in the same way, except that they are planted in the second

CHITTING POTATO TUBERS

Chitting simply means encouraging the potato tubers to sprout before planting. The kind of long shoots that appear when potatoes have been stored in the dark for some time are no use – the shoots must be short and sturdy. Place the tubers in a tray in a light position, perhaps by a window, where there is no risk of frost.

Chitting is useful if you want the tubers to get off to a quick start, as they will usually emerge from the ground a week or two before unchitted tubers.

Before planting, place the potatoes in a tray in a light place (but out of direct sunlight) in order to "chit". This means that the potatoes produce shoots.

half of spring and the potatoes are set 38cm/15in apart and in rows 60cm/24in apart for second earlies and 75cm/30in apart for maincrop.

It is safe to plant potatoes in most areas, as it will take several weeks before the frost-sensitive shoots emerge from the soil, and these can be protected by earthing up the plants. In cold areas, however, it is best to chit your potatoes and delay planting for a couple of weeks or so. It is a good idea to use cloches, floating cloches or horticultural fleece in areas where frost is still likely.

An alternative method of growing potatoes is to plant them under a sheet of black plastic. Place the plastic sheet along the row and anchor it by burying the edges in the soil. Cut slits at the relevant intervals and plant the potatoes through them.

PLANTING IN THE OPEN

1 Use a draw hoe, spade or rake head to make wide flat-bottomed or V-shaped drills 10–13cm/4–5in deep. Space the rows about 45cm/18in apart for early varieties, 60cm/24in for second earlies, and 75cm/30in for the maincrop.

2 Space the tubers about 30–45cm/ 12–18in apart in the rows. Make sure that the shoots or eyes (buds about to grow into shoots) face upwards. For larger tubers, leave only three sprouts on each one and rub the others off.

3 Carefully cover the tubers by pulling the excavated soil back into the drill. Potatoes must be earthed (hilled) up as they grow to prevent the tubers from turning green and to protect the shoots from frost damage.

PLANTING UNDER A PLASTIC SHEET

1 If you do not want the effort of earthing up your potatoes, plant them under a black plastic sheet. Bury the edges in the soil and cover with loose soil to anchor the sheets.

2 Use a sharp knife to make rows of cross-shaped slits in the plastic where the tubers are to be planted.

3 Plant the tubers through the slits, using a trowel. Make sure that each tuber is covered with 3–5cm/1–2in of soil. As they grow the shoots will find their way through the slits.

Growing in rows

Potatoes have traditionally been grown in rows. Although some gardeners challenge the claims made for this method, suggesting that blocks and deep beds are better, rows are probably still the most widely used system.

The basic idea for growing any vegetables in rows is simple: they are grown in a single line, with some crops, such as beans, being grown in a double line. The rows are separated by a distance somewhat wider than the breadth of the plants, so that there is space between the rows. This bare earth acts as a path, allowing access for weeding, watering and harvesting.

ADVANTAGES

Growing potatoes and other vegetables in rows is an attractive way of producing them. The varying heights, shapes, textures and colours show up well, with the rows looking like ribbons stretched across the garden. As well as growing in this way for the sake of appearance, there are practical considerations, too.

Access is one of the important benefits provided by individual rows. The paths between the rows allow the gardener to move freely among the plants to examine them. Pests have less chance of being overlooked if the plants can be clearly seen from at least two sides, and individual plants can be tended if necessary. The bases of the plants can be easily seen for inspection, weeding and watering.

ABOVE Growing potatoes in rows looks attractive and allows the gardener access for weeding, watering and examining the plants for pests and diseases.

Another advantage is that there is plenty of air circulating among the plants, which helps considerably to reduce mildew-type diseases. The plants generally have plenty of space in which to develop, and the leaves are able to open out to receive the maximum amount of light. Finally, rows are easier to cover with cloches.

DISADVANTAGES

Needless to say, there are also disadvantages to growing in rows. The use of so many paths means that a lot of space is unproductive when you look at the plot as a whole, an important factor in a small garden. Another disadvantage is that the paths allow light to reach the soil, so increasing the number of weeds that germinate, although this is offset to some extent by the ease with which it is possible to hoe.

With constant use, the paths become compacted, which does not help the soil structure. Although the whole bed will be dug each year, because the area is so large it is necessary to walk over it while the ground is being prepared, again adding a certain degree of compaction. Constant hoeing will break up the soil and keep it aerated, but in dry weather hoeing should be avoided as it encourages water loss.

An alternative is to lay planks of wood between the rows. This not only helps to prevent soil compaction, but also acts as a mulch, which will help retain the moisture in the soil as well as keep the weeds down.

Growing in containers

Increasing interest is being shown in containers as a method of growing potatoes in a small space, perhaps on the patio or possibly even on a balcony or roof garden. A wide range of beautiful containers are now available from garden centres and nurseries, many of which will accommodate potatoes.

THE CONTAINERS

Virtually any container can be used to grow potatoes, but success is more likely if it is reasonably large – the bigger the better, in fact. Potatoes do not like to dry out, and the greater the volume of compost (soil mix) that is available, the less chance there is of this occurring. Terracotta pots are extremely attractive, but the porous nature of the material allows water to evaporate more quickly through the sides of the pot than through a glazed or plastic one. Most pots are heavy even without compost, so make sure you position them before you fill them. Large, black plastic buckets with holes in the bottom are practical and can be used successfully, although they are not as attractive as ceramic pots.

THE POSITION

Containers of potatoes can be placed together with purely decorative containers, although they should not be grown in shade. Bear in mind that plants grown in pots do not have the solid mass of earth around their roots to keep them cool during the day, and it is possible that the roots can become too hot. Another problem with siting the containers in a warm place is that they will need watering several times a day.

You should, therefore, choose a warm but not hot place, preferably one where there is plenty of air circulating, but not exposed to strong winds.

From a decorative point of view, potatoes can be grown wherever they will fit in. A group of containers can make an attractive feature on a patio.

PLANTING, GROWING AND HARVESTING

Fill the base of the barrel or pot with a generous layer of compost (approximately a quarter full). Arrange the potatoes 15cm/6in apart on the surface of the compost. Cover with another layer of compost until the container is no more than approximately half full. Water thoroughly after planting and continue to water whenever the compost shows any sign of drying out. A weak liquid fertilizer may be applied if manure is not available.

When the leaves appear and reach about 10cm/4in in height, add another layer of compost to cover them completely. Repeat this process until the pot is completely full of compost. Continue to water the plants regularly.

The plants are ready to harvest once they have flowered. Dig up the plants carefully using a fork or trowel. Only dig up as many potatoes as you need. The others will keep better if they remain in the soil until you want them.

ABOVE The potatoes should be arranged 15cm/6in apart in the container on a layer of compost (soil mix).

ABOVE Dig up the potatoes you need, leaving the remainder in the soil until you want them.

Harvesting and storing

Early potatoes are usually lifted as soon as they are required, but maincrop potatoes are generally left in the soil until autumn, when they are lifted all at once and stored.

HARVESTING

Potatoes are usually ready to be harvested just as the flowers are opening, which is about three months after planting. Whenever possible, harvest potatoes on a dry, warm day to avoid blight, and handle the tubers gently so that they are not bruised.

To check if earlies are ready, push away a little earth from the top of the ridges and remove any tubers that are ready to eat. Replace the soil to allow the smallest potatoes to continue to grow. To harvest the whole plant, dig a fork in well below the potatoes and lever them carefully out of the soil, at the same time pulling on the haulms (the top growth, the stems and leaves). With maincrop potatoes, remove the haulm about two weeks before harvesting so that the skins will harden slightly.

ABOVE Potatoes have very attractive flowers. The clusters of small, white star-shaped flowers have yellow anthers. This ornamental quality is an added bonus in the kitchen garden. In early crops, the opening of the flowers is an indication that the tubers are ready.

LIFTING, DRYING AND SORTING

1 Lift the tubers with a fork once the foliage has died down. You can leave them in the ground for longer if penetrating frosts are not likely to be a problem, but lift promptly if pests such as slugs appear.

2 Leave the potatoes on the surface for a couple of hours so that the skins dry off and harden before sorting and storing them.

3 Sort the potatoes before storing. It is sufficient to grade them into four sizes: very small, small, medium and large. Discard or use up very small ones immediately, keep small ones for use soon, and store the medium and largest.

1 Place medium and large potatoes in paper sacks to store in a cool, frost-proof place.

2 Alternatively, make a clamp in the garden. Excavate a shallow depression and line it with a thick layer of straw.

3 Pile the potatoes on to the bed of straw, as shown.

4 Heap a thick layer of straw over the top. It must be thick enough to provide good insulation.

5 Mound earth over the straw, but leave a few tufts of straw sticking out of the top for ventilation.

6 If you have a dry, dark and frost-free garage, you can store potatoes in open racks.

Lift the crop on a dry day and leave them lying in the open for an hour or two to dry and encourage the skins to harden still more. Do not leave any tubers in the ground: they will rot and introduce pests and diseases to the soil.

STORAGE

Never leave potatoes in the light for too long or they will begin to turn green, when they must be discarded. Pack them into paper or hessian (burlap) sacks and store them in a dark, cool but frost-free place. Alternatively, they can be stored in trays as long as no light can get to the tubers. Check all potatoes regularly and remove any that show signs of rot or scab.

Early and mid-season potatoes are best eaten as soon as possible. The later growing maincrops are generally stored for winter use. The warmth of a centrally heated kitchen can cause potatoes to start sprouting, the dampness of a cold refrigerator will make them sweaty and mouldy, and in too much light they will lose their nutritional value and start to turn green. If you have only a small number, they are best kept in paper sacks indoors, or in a rack, basket or well-ventilated bin in a dry, dark place. For a large crop, try using a traditional clamp, which may look primitive but works unless you live in an area that has very severe winters.

Common problems

Whether you grow potatoes in a container or in the vegetable plot, they require little attention apart from watering, weeding, feeding and covering with earth. The most usual problems can be avoided if a few precautions are taken.

ACCIDENTAL DAMAGE

One of the most common problems with potatoes is the damage caused by the over-enthusiastic gardener who accidentally pierces or slices tubers when lifting them. When the crop is ready for harvesting, begin to dig a good distance from the main stem and if possible use a flat-tined fork, which will be less likely to damage the tubers if you do accidentally spear one.

DROUGHT

A prolonged period of drought followed by a sudden downpour can cause tubers to split, making them susceptible to pests and diseases. Enhancing the moisture-retaining properties of the ground will help. You can either dig in plenty of well-rotted organic material before planting, or lay a mulch afterwards. It is also important to water regularly throughout the growing season so that the plants are not checked as they develop.

FROST

The sudden browning and wilting of leaves overnight is usually caused by frost. Because first early potatoes are planted in early spring, with second earlies planted out just a couple of weeks later, the young shoots might be damaged by late frosts. In cold weather protect the plants at night with straw, sacking or hessian (burlap), or horticultural fleece. Even laying sheets of newspaper over young plants can be sufficient to prevent frost from damaging the plants.

If you are growing maincrop potatoes, early autumn frosts can be a problem. Again, when frosts are forecast, protect plants with horticultural fleece or newspaper.

PROTECTION AND INSULATION

Covering plants with straw gives them extra protection when winter weather becomes severe.

Cloches can be used to protect crops through the winter or as temporary cover in spring whenever frosts threaten.

Newspaper makes an excellent temporary insulation against sudden frosts in spring. Drop several layers, one on top of the other, to create air pockets. Do not leave on during the day.

Fleece has a similar function to newspaper. It is very light and will not harm the plants. Unlike newspaper, it can be left on during the day as light penetrates through it.

GREENING

Potato tubers that are exposed to sunlight turn green and cannot be eaten. For this reason, potato plants need to be earthed (hilled) up regularly as they grow.

Closely grown potatoes will eventually shade themselves, as the foliage meets across the rows, and potatoes grown under black plastic do not need to be covered, of course.

WEEDS

Unwanted plants not only take nutrients and moisture from the soil, depriving vegetables of their share, but they can also harbour diseases, which can be passed on to your crops. Keep your potato plot clear of weeds if you want to produce the best vegetables.

Hoeing off weed seedlings as they appear will take only a few minutes. Allow them to become fully grown and it will take hours to remove them.

EARTHING UP

1 Start earthing (hilling) up the potatoes when the shoots are about 15cm/6in high. Use a draw hoe to pull up the soil on either side of the row.

2 Continue to earth up in stages, as the potatoes grow. You should end up with mounds of soil alongside each plant that are about 15cm/6in high.

WEEDING

It is not always possible to hoe without damaging the vegetables, or because the weeds are too well advanced. Weeding with a hand fork is then the best alternative.

Avoid using chemical weedkillers in the vegetable garden. If necessary, use them to kill persistent weeds when initially preparing the plot. Always follow the manufacturer's instructions.

Pests and diseases

Lists of the potential pests and diseases can so alarm gardeners that they decide not to try growing potatoes at all. This is a shame, for as long as crop rotation is practised (never growing potatoes in the same place two years running) and plants are protected from slugs and snails, potatoes are among the most reliable croppers of all vegetables.

APHIDS

Greenfly and blackfly (sometimes other colours) infest the stems and young leaves. This is not a serious problem as long as the insects do not transmit a viral disease, which will affect tubers kept for use as seed potatoes. Heavy infestations may cause leaves to curl round. Spray with insecticidal soap, bifenthrin, permethrin or pyrethrum in the evening.

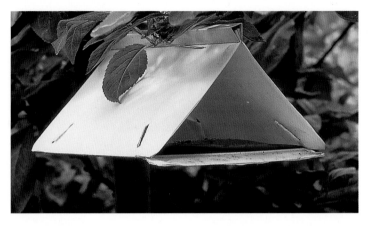

BLACKLEG

This bacterial problem appears early in the season. The rolled foliage turns yellow, and shoots blacken and collapse as the base of the stem rots. If tubers are infected they develop a brown, slimy rot. Lift and burn all infected plants.

Avoid the problem by growing on well-drained land and make sure that all tubers are lifted at the end of the season.

BLIGHT

The most serious potato disease, the fungus affects leaves, stems and tubers. Yellowish-brown patches appear on the leaves, and in dry weather they become dry and brown. In wet weather the leaves, then the stems, turn black and rot and a white fungal growth appears under the leaves. Infected tubers have dark, slightly sunken patches on the skin, and a reddish-brown discoloration may spread to the flesh. Potato blight will spread quickly in warm, humid weather.

ABOVE Sticky traps are a good form of non-spray control that is becoming popular for a wide range of pests. Here, pheremones attract insect pests to the trap, where they get stuck.

Once infected, the only cure is to cut off all the top growth and burn it. Leave the tubers in the ground and harvest them three weeks later. Avoid the problem by planting potatoes at least 13cm/5in deep, and careful earthing (hilling) up, which helps to prevent the spores entering the soil even when leaves are infected.

CYST EELWORM

The leaves of affected plants turn yellow and dry from the bottom up, and plants die prematurely. There is no cure available, and because the eggs can remain viable in the cysts for more than 10 years, crop rotation can only help to prevent the build-up of the cysts. It may be necessary to stop growing potatoes for several years.

ABOVE Help to avoid infection by lifting potatoes in dry weather and making sure that no tubers are left in the ground. Store only those tubers that are healthy.

POTASH DEFICIENCY

The deficiency will be noticed when the edges of the oldest leaves turn brown and curl, with a scorched appearance. A liquid feed of comfrey (made by leaving comfrey leaves in water to rot) will help in the short term, but to prevent the problem recurring, improve the soil by adding well-rotted compost and seaweed meal.

ROT

Potatoes are affected by two types of rot: dry rot and gangrene. Dry rot affects tubers in store, and it causes the skins of affected tubers to become wrinkled at one end. The wrinkles form circles and become discoloured. Pinkish, white or bluish-green fungal growth can be seen. Avoid the problem by lifting and handling the mature tubers carefully and storing them in a cool but frost-free place.

Gangrene affects tubers soon after they are lifted. Sunken patches appear, and the skin may become wrinkled. Affected tubers rot, turn wet and pale pink and finally darker. Avoid the problem by lifting tubers carefully. Check tubers in store regularly and discard any that show signs of rot.

SCAB

Two forms of scab affect potatoes: common and powdery. Common scab, a fungal infection, causes roughened, raised patches on the skin of tubers. Although the flesh is not always damaged, it may crack and become discoloured. The fungus causing common scab is

naturally present in soil, but the problem is worse on light, sandy, alkaline soils. Dig grass mowings into the planting trench, mulch with well-rotted compost to improve the soil and water regularly. Do not lime the soil before planting, and if the soil is very alkaline, consider adding sulphate of ammonia or superphosphate to reduce the pH. There is no fungicidal treatment available to amateur gardeners.

Potatoes with powdery scab, another fungal problem, have small, round scabby patches on the skin. The scabs burst and release brown spores into the soil. Burn infected tubers and do not use the same site for potatoes for at least three years.

SLUGS AND SNAILS

In late summer slugs make circular holes in tubers and may create large cavities inside the potatoes. Scatter pellets (metaldehyde or methiocarb) or spray with liquid metaldehyde. Alternatively, use a biological control (nematodes). Dig up tubers promptly to prevent damage.

Slugs and snails also eat the above-ground parts of plants. Cultivate the land to expose the eggs to predators. Go out at night with a torch (flashlight) and collect the pests, or sink saucers of beer in the ground to drown them.

You might also try strewing surplus seedlings or leaves around young potato plants so that the slugs and snails will be attracted to the waste material and not the crops themselves.

SPRAING

This problem is caused by viruses spread by nematodes. The flesh of affected potatoes has reddish lines or circles and may be corky. Stems and leaves of infected plants may have yellow mottling, and tubers may be distorted. Remove affected plants. Avoid the problem by making sure that you do not plant hosts of tobacco rattle virus, such as sweet (bell) pepper, hyacinth, gladiolus, tulip, China aster or tobacco plants near your potatoes.

WIREWORM

Narrow but extensive tunnels are made in tubers by the larvae of click beetles, which are a problem in grassed areas that have recently been brought into cultivation. The problem usually disappears once ground has been cultivated for four or five years, during which time the larvae will have been exposed to birds.

In the meantime, lift tubers as soon as they are ready. Water in pirimiphos-methyl or treat the soil at the start of the growing season with lindane or chlorpyrifos and diazinon.

ABOVE Slugs and snails have few friends among gardeners. They make holes in just about any part of a plant, often leaving it useless or even dead.

Growing potatoes organically

As increasing numbers of people become concerned about the levels of artificial insecticides, fungicides and weedkillers used in the commercial production of all vegetables and fruit, the attractions of organically grown produce are becoming self-evident. Potatoes are an ideal crop to grow organically.

ORGANIC GARDENS

There is more to organic gardening than just not using chemicals. Organic gardeners work to improve the quality of the soil to provide plants with the best possible growing conditions. They also aim to develop a natural balance within the garden by attracting wildlife to help combat pests and to pollinate plants, and by growing a wide range of plants. In this way attacks by pests and diseases affect only a small proportion of the entire vegetable plot, and the inclusion of companion plants acts as a positive deterrent to some forms of pest.

In the vegetable garden do not plant potatoes with tomatoes and kohlrabi, because these plants are susceptible to many of the same diseases and predators. Including clumps of French marigolds (*Tagetes*), which have a distinctive, pungent scent, in the vegetable garden has been shown to have a useful deterrent effect on aphids.

Rather than single or double digging the vegetable plot on a regular basis, some organic gardeners prefer the no-dig system. After an initial thorough digging to remove all perennial weed roots and other debris, the soil is gradually built up by the annual addition of mulches of well-rotted compost and manure. Worms and soil-borne organisms take the nutrients down in the soil; the gardener does not dig in the material. Because the ground is not disturbed by digging, the soil is not unnecessarily aerated (which increases the rate at which nutrients can leach out) and the natural layers of soil that develop over time are not destroyed. No-dig beds are usually found as raised beds or as areas of the vegetable garden that are surrounded by permanent or semi-permanent paths so that the soil is never compacted.

LEFT Potatoes grow very well in chemical-free organic gardens, in which the soil is gradually built up by the addition of mulches of well-rotted compost and manure. These freshly harvested potatoes will make delicious "new potatoes".

GREEN MANURE

In addition to regular applications of well-rotted compost or manure, organic gardeners often sow green manures in ground that has become vacant as a crop is cleared after harvesting. These plants, which include alfalfa, some types of beans and peas and *Phacelia tanacetifolia*, are dug into the ground before they have set seed and are valuable for fixing nitrogen in the soil.

One of the most useful and decorative green manures is a pretty hardy annual, the poached-egg plant (*Limnanthes douglasii*), which can be sown in autumn (when the potatoes have been cleared away) and will produce a good weed-suppressing ground cover of leaves, which can be dug in the following spring, before the flowers appear. The flowers will self-seed readily.

BIOLOGICAL CONTROLS

Whenever predators appear, organic gardeners choose not to spray their crops with insecticides and other chemicals. Biological controls, which are increasingly widely available, are the ideal way of controlling many common pests. They usually work best when the weather is warm, although some are not suitable for outdoor use.

Introduce them as soon as the first signs of attack are noticed, and do not use any insecticides at all once a biological control has been introduced. Be patient and accept that there will be some damage before the biological agent takes

ABOVE A good mixed garden, with plenty of varieties of flowers and vegetables, is less likely to have problems than one restricted to a monoculture. It will attract insects, which in turn attack pests.

RIGHT Green manure helps to improve both the structure and fertility of the soil. Sow it when the ground is not being used for anything else and then dig it in before it flowers and sets seed.

effect. When you use biological controls there will always be some pests – they are essential for the predator to continue to breed – but the population will be reduced.

Index

The publisher would like to
thank the following for supplying
pictures: The Garden Picture
Library 60b; The Harry Smith
Collection 56t; Peter McHoy 62.